Birth of Light

Michael Nelder Henderson III

Published by: The Auditory Museum

ISBN: 978-1-7356710-0-0 (paperback)

ISBN: 928-1-7356710-1-7 (e-book)

dedicated to 16-year-old me, trying to find his uniqueness

CONTENTS

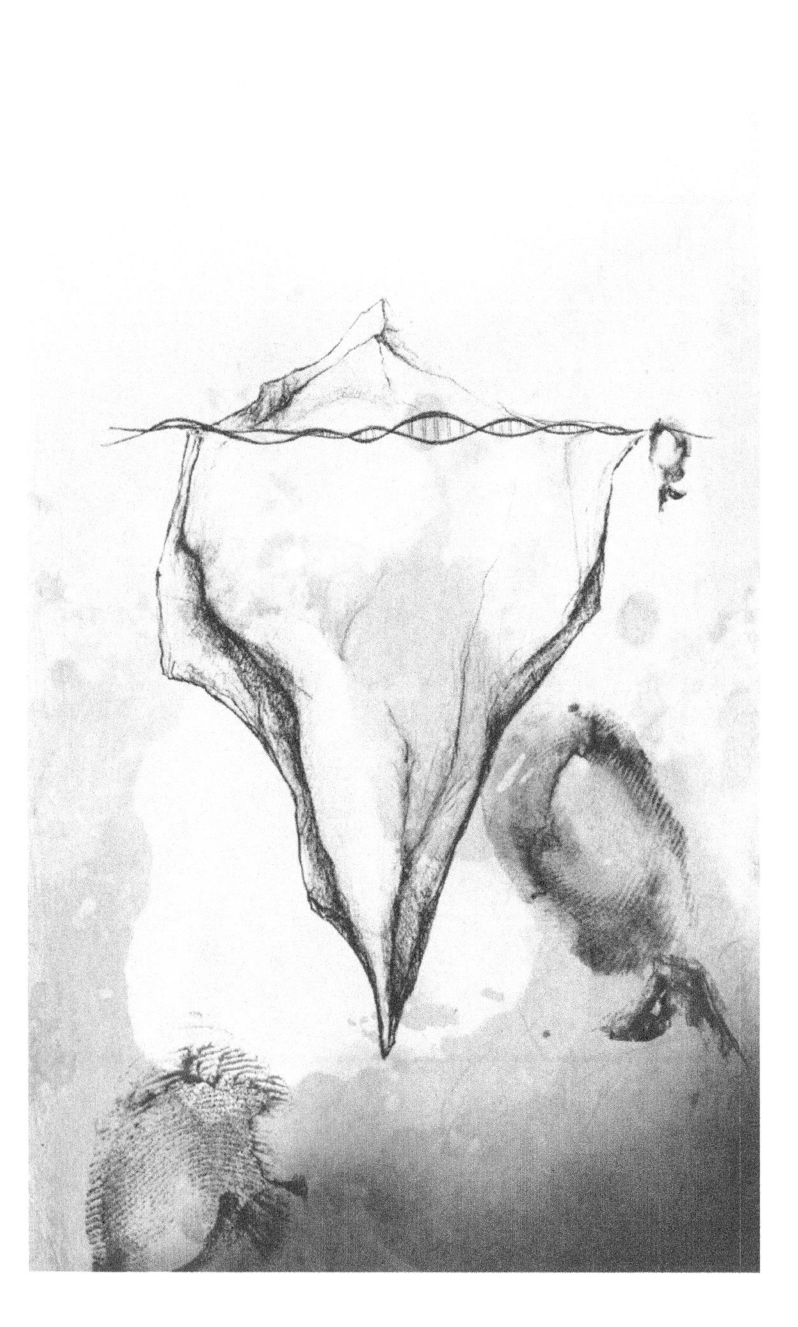

HOLES

I like
to remind
my fear

that lightening
is just spaghetti

shooting out
of the sky.

-Landscape

He writes
when God ignores him,
lifting his pen
in worship
to force
his holy words
on unworthy broken
notebook pages,
sewn together
in doubt.

He reads them
like the Bible.
Often blind
in braille, he carries
the Book of Eli.

“And my man,”
I am not saying
I am Denzel...I wish.
And I’m definitely not saying
I am God.

You just have
to understand
he has always
spoken best to me
through poetry...

-He Writes

I am not
a sore throat.

I am the sound
of a heart attack
on the other end
of a stethoscope
reminding the sick
that there is still
hope for humanity
as long as
one man's heart
continues to struggle
for truth.

I am not
a collection
of good quotes
that need validation
from vain lines.

I am a journal
of suicide bombings
and blasted windows
that only give
way to real words
after I have slaughtered
my insecurities.

-Testimonial

I wonder
what happens
every time
I erase a line.

If somehow, it appears
in a book that God
keeps in his back pocket
to be opened
on judgement day
and read aloud
to all of heaven.

-Abandoned by Fear

My friend
once told me
I am a womanizer
of dreams and ideas.

-Womanizer of Dreams

we write,
we revise,
we wrestle
we rehearse,
we film,
we hustle,
we repeat.

-Unholy

he writes
to be a lifesaver,
chest pumping
"you're worthy's"
and "you are
more than ables"
into the mental lungs
of those who
have never breathed
their own air.

he writes to kiss uniqueness,
to remember
for every one
person on earth,
there are six galaxies
full of one hundred
million stars...

-He Writes More

I want to ask
my parents
what kind of love
has the ability
to birth a ship
inside of a bottle,

which is to say:
I have always felt
like a vessel
inside of a vessel,

made to be carried
while responsible
for unmarked truth
in its bowels.

-Love Vessel

my friend Jeff
asked me where
I saw myself in 5 years
and I said,
"what if it's less about
where I want to be
and more about
how I need to feel?"

then he drew rolling hills
on a napkin and told me,
"this is how you
experience emotions, huh…
your highs are really high
but your lows are really low,"

and I started crying
until he flipped
the same napkin
upside down and said,
"what if you got it all wrong?
what if your valleys
are really your peaks
and what if your peaks
are really your valleys?
or what if it's all the same,
like the neediness of
your soul just mirrors
god's infinite ability to give?"

-Less About

Don't judge me
for stealing
toilet paper
out of the library.

I pay
35,000 dollars
a year in tuition
and the toilet
rolls from the
99 cents store
ain't doing
the trick.

It's hard
out here
and college
has taught me
that if you
want something,
you have
to be willing
to occupy
as many stalls
as possible.

-Yung Sallie

can I start
over as myself?

cause it feels like
I'm locked up
in somebody else.

-Facsimile

If the mirror
didn't matter,
I'd write
for self-expression,

tell you what's
really going on,
wake up
a little earlier,
take myself
our for a walk,
and maybe adopt
a dog and
call him Peter.

He would
represent
a childhood
that ran away.

-Didn't Matter

I've written
a thousand
letters to myself
wondering when
I would be home
to read them.

-Come Back

his notebook pages
aren't afraid
of his blood
disguised as ink.

they accept his…
"I don't know
if I'll be okay..."

like cancer patients
in radiation treatment
carry his last words,
like tombstones
and forgotten
African mausoleums
protect conversations
he could never have
with his mother or father.

-Real Friends

would you
believe me
if I told you

both joy
and grief

weigh the exact
same thing?

-Scales

one day
it'll all
settle

like snow that
has just tasted
the ground.
the inferiority,
the self,
marginalization,
the hiding
in plain sight,
the war
of comparison.

one day
it'll all
settle.

the dressing for
other people's eyes,
the smiles we
use to cosign,
for all the things
we add and subtract
just to make certain
people will accept us.

one day
it'll all
settle.

we'll accept
these browns eye
and stop wanting them greens...
we'll wear
this skin proudly
and stop undoing
the seams.

for once, we'll
close our eyes
and enjoy
the sweet lips
of our dreams.
we'll stop waiting
to be knighted
and declare
ourselves King.

grandmama used
to always say,

"baby… one day,
it'll all settle
in your soul."

-Settle

she said,
“you can
ask me
about life
only after
you've died
to yourself,
like your
ability to feel
is the most
important gift
you haven't
managed
to lose yet.”

-Feelings

I hear their whispers
beneath the sea.
I see the fingerprints
in the sand
and their hands
in the waves.

There is not
a people alive
that know the body
of an ocean
more intimately
than the black skin
that lies underneath it.

Help us to remember,
Help us to remember,
Help us to remember.

-Remember Me

When I was
a little boy,
I would listen
to you preach
and would always hate
to hear you talk
about heaven,
not because I didn't
want to go
but because you said,
"there would be
no such thing
as mothers
and fathers
in heaven."

I couldn't
stand the thought
of you not being
my daddy.

-Pedestal

I need
to know
you're achieving

to let me know
the sacrifices
I made for you
were worth it.

-My Black Mum

my mom is so dope
the ground collects her footprints.
my mom is so dope
cows sacrifice their bodies
so she can cook them
for dinner steaks.

my mom is so dope
she can cook baked potatoes
with her brain waves.

my mom is so dope
dope dealers give her
a percentage of their profits,
which she donates to charity.

my mom is dope
she named herself Angela at birth.

my mom is so dope
even the spit from her mouth
can be used to remove
facial blemishes.

my mom is so dope,
when she touches ashy skin,
it immediately gets moist.

-Mooka

when tears
turned to laughter:
conversations with
my brothers that
I will never forget.

-Thicker

I'm still trying
to remember
where I buried
the treasure...

What map has
the red X
marks the spot
with instructions
written on the back...
"How to
defeat Captain Hook…"

Which lunch table
did I leave
the box of Crayola's
shaped like
square pizzas
and barrel juices from the 90's,
with far more
colors than
adolescence
or adulthood.

-Kids Again

when they ask
what kind
of love
could have
birthed me,

I now know
it was
a love

that had
to feel.

-It Had To

When I was a kid,
I used to always
ask my mom
this one question:
"Mom, is there anything
in this world
that I don't know?"

It’s like my future self knew
it would need the wisdom
to exist while being
a dreamer and a doer
at the same time.

We can't help:
that were dreamers,
that we measure success
by only ever asking
ourselves one question

Did we grow up to be
who we said
we were going to be
when they asked us
as kids?

-Can You Still Make Out the Dream

One day

I'll just do it.
I'll just tell them
I can't come anymore,
I can't make it,
I can't shake it,
I'm not subscribing
to someone
else's dream.

I will follow
my map
and dust will collect
on my desk.

-At Will Resignation

On the day
before I die,
I will collect
every butterfly
I've ever had
in my stomach,
and before
giving them away
to random strangers,
I'd write lessons
I learned
on their wings like:

"The best poets
and people
are the ones
who never learn
how to perform."

-Day Before I Die

My ears
will never forget
Dr. Khamsi Brown's words
after they asked
him about
the greatest gift
he's ever received:

"God has given me
the gift of weeping."

-Without Repentance

WHEN A TREE FALLS

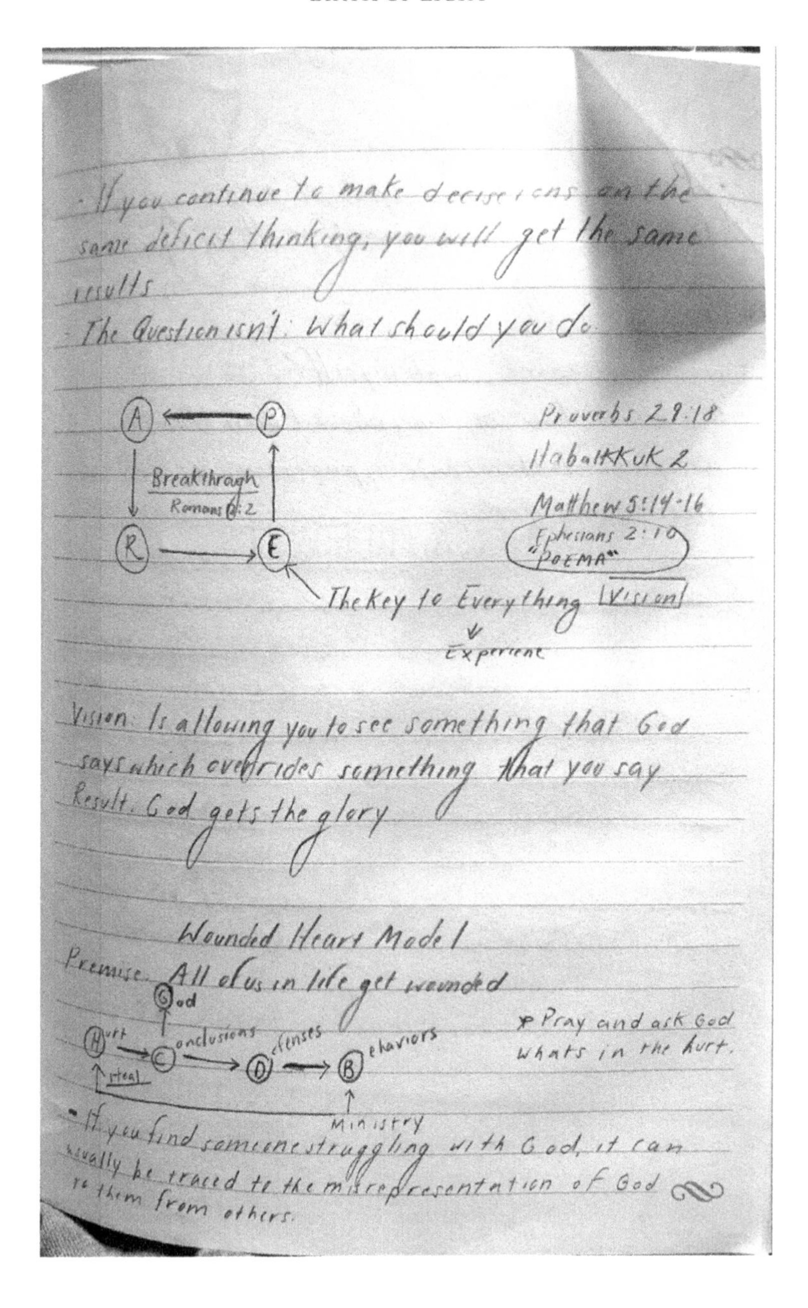

· If you continue to make decisions on the same deficit thinking, you will get the same results.
- The Question isn't: What should you do
A
P
R
E
Breakthrough
Romans 12:2
Proverbs 29:18
Habakkuk 2
Matthew 5:14-16
Ephesians 2:10 "POEMA"
The key to Everything [Vision]
Experience
Vision: Is allowing you to see something that God says which overrides something that you say
Result: God gets the glory
Wounded Heart Model
Premise: All of us in life get wounded
God
Hurt
Conclusions
Defenses
Behaviors
Heal
Ministry
* Pray and ask God whats in the hurt.
• If you find someone struggling with God, it can usually be traced to the misrepresentation of God to them from others.

when a tree falls
in this forest
and nobody
is around
to hear it,
it invites arsonists
to set it on fire…

like it would
willingly allow itself
to be burned alive
along with everything
good inside of it
just to make
a statement:

face-paint sky
in cross-shaped black
signaling ash
Wednesday repentance.
it will perform
acts of sacrilege
just to be heard.

-Blood Soiled

how do I see
my insides
like a shelter
I run to
rather than
a war zone
that I was
born into?

a sanctuary
where I go
to escape
rather than
a murder scene,
‘cause sometimes,

what is inside
scares me
more than
what’s outside.

-Focus on Home

if pain
were a
noose,
we'd all
be hanging,
we'd all
be swinging,
we'd all
be colliding
into each
other's ruin
wondering

what took us
so long
to figure out

we are all
connected
by the same
rope.

-Tug of War

I tell
my therapist
my biggest fear
is hearing
myself speak
because I am
afraid of my voice
not making sense,

afraid of feeling
the kind of messed up
I can't explain away,
can't explain how
I can speak
everyone's language
but can't understand
my own tongue.

I tell him
my words always
end up forming
crop circles
on paper,
so good luck trying
to figure me out.

-Bullies

this boy heals way too fast,
does not allow himself
to feel the scalpel of emotion
so there is no history for his pain.

his skin reeks of masked perfection
and he wonders who will tell his story:
oppressor or oppressed.
he wonders if he is both,
if his life is just inverted privilege;
the ability to talk and never
remember what was said.

he wonders if he has this disease
that makes emotions
become placeholders
rather than pictures.
this boy is afraid of the frames
more than the photos.

if fear grew teeth, it would bite him
in the stories he tells
other people about who he is.
his excuse is always
"the dog ate his homework."

he treats creating scripts
for every occasion like assignments
and stores the scripts he cannot finish
underneath the pillows of lovers.

-Masked Imperfect

do you know how it feels
to yell your voice bloody?

to swallow other people's prayers
with a sore throat?

-Benediction

lonely
is what's happening
when you trade places
with your shadow
and look at
who you were
in the sun.

-The Lost

why am I always trying
to clean up
what's around me?

make it up,
dress it pretty.

is this the dark side
of privilege
or am I a boy

still trying
to win love
he cannot see

surrounds him?

-Distorted

most nights I smoke
until I feel more of me
than incessant thoughts.

most nights I masturbate
to random shit
to get rid of the screaming
attempt to trade god
idols for silence.

-Pain Barters

'we buried you alive,
only find out
there's no receipt
when you give
something precious
to the grave.

you were never
around long enough
for your tombstone
to read anything.
it wasn't fair for us
to make you our savior,

wrap you in flesh
and crucify you
for our weaknesses.
getting lost in each
other made us
lose heaven
and I am afraid
we may never recover.

-Parents Aborted

when she took
the "I" out
of my choice,
all I would have
are your echoes,

distant cries from
street horns
and city sirens
that pass too quickly
for me to hold.

even the city teases
me about your death.

-Abortion Grievances

All I ever wanted
was the love
of my father,
served continental breakfast
Best Western style.

I never needed
a silver platter,
I just wanted
to be taken seriously.

You told me
you suffered
from depression
and I decided
not to believe you.
I denied you like people
deny the holocaust,
pretended like slavery
never existed because God
is not allowed to suffer.

-Father May I

"a tree never forgets,"
my dad would say,
he has never forgotten
being afraid of his father.

my grandfather
would say he ran away
to the navy at 17
because he was
afraid of his father.

they would both
tell me they suffered
from depression,
and I am learning
you can quickly
understand a forest
by examining its roots,
but it doesn't
necessarily mean
the trees will grow
any differently,

especially when
they've only
ever tasted blood
from the soil.

-Blood Soiled

I am afraid
to start anything
because I am still
waiting for you
to finish with me.

I never thought
I'd be the one
having to protect
superman.

I turned into a villain
believing you
were my hero

-Black Dads

a father figure tells me,
"learning how to perform
was the survival you mastered
to get through school

to make sure other kids
couldn't torture you anymore
like their parents tortured them.
now, we just have to find
your face in all these masks."

-Nostalgia Sick

tell them,
the only way
to kill loneliness
is in moments
and in pieces
when you're able
to capture it
on paper.

-Lure

it's hard for me to rest
when everything inside
beats so fast.
it’s hard for me to accept love
when all I've ever known
are heart attacks
and heart failures,
cardiac arrests... you see,
I'm not used to being healthy.
I just make sure
everyone thinks I am

but who am I?
I always ask the question:
why can’t this fearful heart
accept your
reckless invitation?

-Up from the Ashes

even though
they are
abandoned ruins,

they are still
your memories.

-Oceanside

I am learning
to say "it hurt me"
without finishing
the sentence,

to say, “father
forgive them
for they know
not what they do”
while acknowledging
that the voices still
linger sometimes,
that I still turn into
that high school boy
who gets super defensive
when someone's jokes
come too close
to open wounds.

-Stick and Stones

I catch moments
with notepad and pen,
cage them in memories,
walk them through stories,
feed them with
laughter and tears—
the rare ones always
get extra laughter...

and this is how
I keep process alive
in a world where
moments die too soon,
all because people
are moving
way too fast.

be still.

-Great Grandma

I need some time to do me,
I need some time to see me,
I need some time to love me,
I need some time to trust me,
I need some time to grow me,
I need some time to know me,
I need some time to hold me,
I need some time to chase me,
I need some time to mold me,
I need some time to make me,
I need some time to create me,
I need some time to change me,
I need some time to free me,
I need some time to be me,
I need some time to be me.

-Need Some Time

to freedom,
to chain-less.
you will kick,
scream, claw
your way into the
holy of holies,
rip the veil that
serves as your mask,
fight your way through
crowds of incessant thoughts.

you will slay this dragon
with 1000 heads,
sprout tattered wings
and ascend high,

even though
there is still
a syringe stuck
in your arm,
flying junkies
still addicted
to your suffering,
comfortable in your pain.

you just have to realize,
you're not afraid of death,
you're afraid to be alive.

-You Will Make It No Matter What

you don't even know
where you're going.
someone just told you
it was up,

and you've
already been down,
broken and bloody
bruised and beaten,
chipped-toothed
and unashamed.

your smile will
undoubtedly have
holes from wrestling
with angels.

-The Resilient

loneliness
always happens
just before
the hurt
and the healer
collide.

-The Healer

UNCONSCIOUSLY INCOMPETENT

There is
no more
pressing pain
than a lover
in wait.

-Someday Maybe

we need
another walk:

your mind
and mine.

-TLC

she taught my lips
how to anoint her face.

her forehead
is a perfect backdrop
for grace pressed
against fear.

-Forehead Kiss

always know
the difference
between what you lust after
versus what you long for,

what you reach for
versus what you truly desire.

-Appetites

an old lover tells me,

“after we finished,
you asked me to hold you

I tried to break from your arms
and you begged me to stay.”

I cried disillusionment.
I couldn't remember
my soul telling on itself.

-Conflicting

how did I figure
being lost in her
would help me
find myself?

-Baptism

How does loving you
mean sharing
in the way
you numb

in the cuts
you make
to feel yourself.

-Enabler

I don't remember
when it happened,
when the voices
went from warm to cold,

when we went
from laughing
to defending,
from being
to pointing.

there was silence
in the moments
between the shift.

-Conversation Is Relationship

you are a desert mirage,
a ghostly apparition,
Deja vu that mocks
at 7am and 11:45pm religiously.

I have smelled you before—
my momma mixed with your Uganda.
I've seen you in faint memories
I now call middle passages.

I felt the brush of your face
over my canvas.
you loved to paint
over my pale skin.
we would mix colors
until you left war on my cheeks.

then we'd make up reasons
to stay in bed just a little longer,
sharing the kinds of secrets
only little kids
know how to whisper about,
the kind of secrets grown ups
fall in love just to protect.

I can hear your voice ringing
while my heart beats alarms
I do not know how to silence.
I am still wondering
what was stolen inside.

you despise me
for pushing you away
and I refused to let you
be an accessory to my crimes.

*-F*ck Long Distance*

when the laughter broke,
it was all lost and love,
all war on glass.
every hand was silenced,
every door was damned.

sweet desperate slaves
crave for the day,
for the moment their silence
can be sold on the black market—
black market science,
black jealous act,
break black the chains.

-Heavy

I wish I would've seen
the cruel curse

hidden in her words,

the haunting nature
of the one you love,

who has no intention
of loving you back.

-I Guess?

It was never
about how you tasted,
it more about how you settled
into a stomach
that is a void.

do you know what happens
when a star collapses
in upon itself?

-Black Holes

remember:

in this age
of social media,
the loudest love
isn't always
the deepest.

-Followers

stop being
so afraid of time.

treat it like
a spaceship
and a black light,
knowing it will
either promote her
or expose him.

-Hotline Bling

we all numbing,
trying to feel.
we all have our drug of choice.

you pick the movie.
I like adult films.
what sins do we share?

you told me girls like you—
don't want to be put on the shelf,
always admired but never touched.

I write these poems
for your love.
lay the options by your bed.
what happens when the internet
is dead and we unplug?

will you read the notes
I wrote you
back in high school?

-Bedside Dream

maybe I have always
had a problem
with accepting
god's love

or maybe
you are just
a beautiful painting
I admire
but don't care
to own.

-Experiments

I treat relationships
like I'm this savior
who would die
to protect
the broken one,

like a reason
to give God a break
or when I secretly
want a break from God.

-Finding Home

what if when turning away
and trying to find
this right person
for a distorted version
of happily ever after,

we are subjecting ourselves
to something less than
the divine has for us,
based on our low standards?

-Love Better

I wish I knew
who carved
my heart with
a lightning bolt,
how attraction
always turns into
a firework show
and then disappears.

-Two-Faced

the other day,
I took a love test.
it called me a vacillator.
it said, because my parent
was emotionally unavailable,
I search for connection
and have unrealistic expectations
of the significant others I meet.

my deepest fear
is that I will
never be significant,
that my heart is a black hole,
seeking but never satisfied,
pulling people close
and then shutting down
the oxygen supply.

-Oh Assessments

a wise man
once told me,

“the definition
of conflict
is the distance
between expectations
and reality.”

-Are You Sure

instead of finding
what's wrong with her,
how bout finding
what's right with her
like God does with us?

do I carry the gospel
of men who never get
what they want
or is my appetite
never satisfied?

always expecting
a better version.
comparison robs
me blind all over.

-Something Else

we are
two people
on the border
of two different
countries
staring at
each other
through the holes
in the metal fence
trying to
figure out
why our hands
are touching.

you are
a reflection
to someone
who has never
seen a mirror.

-Where Is This Place?

You had a New York mouth,
the kind that builds cities
but hides feelings
underneath the streets.

I would trade
our glances
for shots
of Jameson
and the pomegranate
tea my grandma makes
with maple syrup.

-Really Want You

if it weren't
too late, I would've
invited you
into my heart
like kids do
with their imaginary friends.
I would've shared secrets
with you
that only my
journal knows.

we would've
decided together:
took my mind
and your heart,
took my heart
and your mind
and exchanged
them like
you've always been
the benefit to
my doubt.

you said
you knew me
better than anyone;
it's just hard to believe
when you've
always felt like
you were
your own
best friend,

I always felt like
ideas understood you
better than people did.

if it weren't
too late, I
would have accepted
you at face value.

-Too Late

tell me how to miss
a girl I never see,
how to connect her words
to the defibrillator in my heart,

all we had was one night,
and there are far too many
incessant thoughts.
my mind is master of games,
and losing them means
she fades away,
but I'm not ready
to forget her face
until I see her again.

I steal feelings for us,
store them in the stories
I continue to tell myself
about who she is,
fill in gaps of what
I've forgotten
with things I'm trying to be,
like someone once said,
"you attract who you are,"
so I'm hoping to land
somewhere in the middle
while I keep hope alive
that one day soon,
I will see her again.

-Fade Back

I will keep coming back
and tattoo your memory
on my wrists,
biting them for blood
hoping I hit a vein.

Vain vanity
keeps me walking dead
all this insanity in my head.

She shaved the picture
from my eyes,
took the waves from the air,
the lines from my fingers,
the touch from my tips.

Love is just
silent rage.
Love is just
silent rage.

Love is just
silent rage,

A murderer
in an H&M jacket.

-Silent Rage Babe

it was your love remembered,
when loneliness made me
want to forget the ink smudged
on my cardboard heart:
"Homeless. Will Work. For Food."
I always wondered why no one
could read it, but you
guess the world doesn't care
what's beneath skin anymore,
and everyone's walked out of 7/11
with a brown paper bag before,
but you never tried to change me,
just helped me count the changes…

and that's when I knew,
the only corners I'd ever
have to face alone would be
the ones from your mouth.

god knew I couldn't take
any more signs… 'cause we're only getting older
and the world's getting more complicated;
we make war just to make love.
we know what we're fighting for.

"dysfunctional,"
dad always says,
"most people are together
based solely on
their dysfunctions,"
and maybe it's true—
I'm broken, you're torn,
but this park bench

is a lot less empty
when I'm sitting on it
with you.

-Love Recalled

she gave me the navy blues
in her long flowing dress.
she knows, whenever she chooses
to wear the ocean—
it's my favorite thing.

her lips are my crashing waves.
I want to be the moon for her,
show her light even in darkness.
I am only reflecting the sun in her.

I know sometimes it's hard
to see yourself but
the thing about the moon is
it explains the ocean's tides
through its gravitational pull.

it's no wonder why
you're so attractive,
no wonder why
I call the ocean
off her body in questions
I continue to ask with my eyes.

how far will you go?
do you think you're enough?
will you give me your depth?

experts say 95% of the ocean
is still unexplored.

I want to ask her if she's ever
seen the ocean swallow the moon?

-Black Twilight

"I just want a girl
with substance"

is the same excuse
every guy uses
until he finds
the girl
that has
the same
substance abuse
problems he does.

-Substance Abuse

she treats
my body
like a
rocking chair,
loves to
place herself
between my legs
move back and forth,
slow like pendulum.

all time is ours.
she feels the universe
as we travel
north to south
in slow motion.

her fingers
grip my sides
and admires oak-
stained a little
too young.

she says
she don't trust
anything that's
too perfect,
looks back
at me with smiles,
continues swinging.

I am pushing
so she goes higher,
like I am a playground
and she is
reclaiming herself.

-Juvenile

it’s only
been one day,
and I already think
you are the angel
that God pulled out
of the world’s mouth.
you make the gospel
seem real.

I have never
felt what it's like
to believe,
but it feels
like this ecstasy pill
they called green goblin
at my first rave.

you always encourage
me to tell stories.
you are my second
poem today
when I haven't
spilt blood
in such
a long time.

-JCK U

I'll just take
the roses
from her cheeks
and give her
to them
as proof.

she is
still a garden
where beautiful
things can grow,

and here am I,
taking time
to smell
the roses.

-It's There

I wonder if the pavement
embraced your feet
like it needed.
you to know
it was thankful
because there are
too many who choose
to walk when they
have the ability to run.

If you reminded skyscrapers
that strong foundations
are sometimes the only
reasons why some
get to touch the heavens
while others are
condemned to earth,
It seemed you
were firmly planted.

-Spirit Strong

She is magician
the way she
makes notes
sing from
the cold,

The way
she bundles
them in lamb's fur
and serves them
to me with
her face
underneath.

I have found
the right songs
to sing
in her eyes,
The kind kids
would play
Double Dutch to
on hot summer days
in New York.

Harlem Renaissance hidden
in 8-second Snapchat
videos of
snow mixed
with rhythm
and blues.

And in a large
cloud of smoke...
POOF!

she disappears.

-Snapchat

You are my
good thing.

I wonder
how you are,
how your heart is,
what your beat
sounds like.

I would love to
dance with you:
your feet on
top of mine.
we can move
like an eraser,
forgetting the past.
sometimes the board
needs to be cleaned.
some students
just learn differently.

-Good Thing

I don't
need
to be
for everybody
as long as
I'm for
somebody...

maybe you?

-Be Specific

When I think about
your story, I hold
in relationship
to the lifespan of
my physical body.

I know eternity
must be real
and life
after death
must exist
in you.

-Locate

The
more
you
you
become
the
clearer
you
can
see
love.

-Chasing

WHOLLY SPIRIT

God Questions

1. Why is it so hard for me to believe in God sometimes?
2. Is it ok for me to struggle with my belief in him?
3. How can I be sure it was Him ordering my steps and not just me making right decisions.
4. Did anyone else in the Bible struggle with their belief in God.
5. How Am I able to see God
6. Can you see God
7. How can I truly be sure He's there?
8. Do I have to just believe the evidence

that hes around
9. How do I know it's just not chemicals being released in my brain that makes me feel a certain way.
10. How do I know that the only reason I believe what I believe isn't because I've been been conditioned by my parents
11. Is there physical evidence that Christ really did walk the earth and die for us
12. Is that really love? If we have to burn in a hell if we don't accept him.
13. Why so much opposition?

a funny
thing happens
when we
love ourselves,
like it
wouldn't matter
if the world
was watching
because we understood.

one day,
our children
would need
examples
to live by...

-Trails

tell me
you don't believe

as long as
you can look up
and really say
everything I feel
has been scripted.

tell me
something real
and I'll risk
my freedom
just to hear
what you speak.

-Whisper

I used to
hate God
because I would
memorize facts
like I needed
to prove
to myself and
everybody else
I knew him
but secretly
resented him
when life would
always present
tests with questions
that required
more than one-
word answers.

-*Facts*

I ran at first.
I didn't know how
to accept you
at face value
when the world
kept painting
you distorted,

when I tried
to reconcile
being created
in your image
with my
broken image.

I have wondered
if seeing
is really believing
or if love
is just a code word
for control.

-Mind Out

Sometimes
I wonder
how my prayers
measure up
to the
next person's,
if my words
carry any
real weight

as compared
to the Syrian boy
across the world,
I have never
felt the gravity
of anything.

I wonder what
he prays for
compared to
what makes me
drop to my knees.
if he prays
safely in
a war-torn country
for family
that will more
than likely
be murdered

while I pray for
high definition
flat screen

television
just so I
could watch
How to Get
Away With
Murder.

It would seem
I get away
with murder

every time
I pray these
privileged
American prayers...

-Dirty Prayers

you must know,

we are not
that strong,
we are not that successful.

at best
we are all
just survivors
somehow surviving,

hanging on
to tiny threads
of grace
we often mistake

for ropes
we've made.

-Swings

is it God
who needs
work or
my idea
of God
that needs
work?

I can't
say today
I believe

but help
my unbelief.

-Unsure World

there is
a kid
in me
but there
is also
a king
in me.

-Seizing Him

the mountains,
your highchair.

the sky,
your theater.

-Understood

"I just want
to feel again,"
said the numb man.
"I just want
to be affected,
overtaken,
overwhelmed.
help me die,
drowning in
your love
so I can
resurrect
in your light,

for my eyes
have gotten
so used
to dark places.

all I see
are shadows
of the child
I once was.

-Before Forgotten

my pastor tells me
I am afraid—
pussy, money and weed
will be your downfall.

the devil wins
if you let him
trick you
into accepting
what's good
in exchange for
your birthright.

is this
something
all pastors say?

I write
not to find me.

I write not
to lose
what's left.

-Outside Eyes

I sit from the sidelines,
watching you jump every hurdle
and traverse every mountain.
you take every one of my excuses
and turn them into reasons
why I should trust you,

why you see me,
how you hear every heartbeat,
loud and clear like an anthem.

my whole life
I've been calling to you
and didn't even know it.

I closed my eyes
to open them in the clouds.

you've always been there,
for some reason
I just couldn't see you.

I am awake enough
to meet you
in the field.

-Marathon

when
my soul
is still,
I can see
the ripples
in the water.

-Outflow

tell me
how you
still burn.

the whirlwind
almost blew
you out.

I need
to know
what keeps
you going,

how you
continue
to be.

To Be Continued...

he speaks and we glance
at each other through the bars,
trying to find the one
that will serve as freedom.

we never found it;
he just served me
his words instead.

Michael, you have to know
when you accept God,
you will have an enemy for life—
you must write to me
so I can encourage you
in the spirit.

and I am learning
that there are free men
around me
that have
done terrible things
just like Todd
but somehow,

they have been set free
to find themselves
in the confines
of darkness.

-*Angola*

every time I search this
callous heart,

I somehow end up in
desert storm.

I don't know how I keep declaring war
or why my voice cracks,

but I am deeply thirsty—

only you can put out the fire
in my throat.

silence the agony in my chest.

I know you've seen the smoke signals.
I can hear you calling to me

faintly through the wilderness.

-Signals and Signs

at lunch
I uploaded
an Instagram photo,

prayed harder for
people to like it
than I prayed
for my grandma
who just had
a stroke.

what would
it mean
for me not
to advertise
my feelings
of insignificance?

I don't know…

-I Don't Know

some people
get really hurt
when they
find out

other people
are imperfect.

-Halo Effect

before bed,
I prayed to
a woman's image,
masturbated like
I knew every
computer click,
paid for a new
set of chains

to put on
a little girl
who hasn't
even decided
if she likes
bracelets yet—
and here
I am wondering
if her prayers
are worth more
than my loneliness.

if every prayer
in the world
is judged equally
or based on
our societal
context.

-Dirty Prayer 2

if God's grace

is the backdrop
for our questions,

then we must
doubt responsibly.

-Can We

find what is yours.
there is treasure
for everyone.

-Unravel

how do you believe
what you say?

do what you say
you'll do.

-Spirit Direct

power is not always
in acceptance.

you realize
your power
in your ability
to reject,
to protest.

I could not be
another Christian
who outwardly
respected but
inwardly resented

my liberation
in questions.

-Discriminate

Freedom
is enough
for me.

-A Soldier

It's been a long time
since my tongue
has scraped a prayer.

I can't figure out
if I have words to say,
or is it that
I can't feel what
I'm saying anymore?

has too much life
gotten in the space
between my heart
and your voice?

everything is so loud!

my deepest fear:
I'll get to the end
and realize
you were right there
in front of my face
and I couldn't
hear you talking.

-Homecoming

We will
do things together:
watch shooting stars,
sunrises and sunsets,

and you'll laugh
as I try to guess
how many galaxies
are in the universe
or how many
grains of sand
are on the beach.

I won't always
think it's fair
that you get
to know how
many hairs
are on my head
but I'll gladly
accept as I
watch you blow
the cloud across
that sky
all while thinking
to myself
how cool
my best friend is.

-Facts

and then he calls you—
draws a line in the sand
and says, cross over,
but only if you're willing
to leave everything
you think you are
and everything
you think you are not
for something higher,
something indescribable.

the great exchange
the weight of your world,
for the weight of his glory.

take off your shoes,
for you are now standing
on holy ground.

-Something Beautiful

I came here
because I need something
and I am ashamed
of having nothing to offer.

take my loneliness,
my insecurity,
my fears
and exchange them
for your glory.

maybe we've both been
asking for the same things.

maybe it just looks like
showing up,
being the same student
of my story
as you've been
of my heart.

we always thought
we weren't alike.
you couldn't
understand what
I needed.

guess I've been asking
the wrong questions
when it's been you
wanting to give
yourself as a blanket

for all the things
I can’t cover
on my own.

I'm diving in
again or for
the first time...
doesn’t matter.

-A Lot Going On

what would happen
if we accepted
his mercy
over sin's judgement,
if we actually believed
there was nothing
else left to prove,

like our lives
were never meant
to be this stage
where we performed
and performed
with our works
and with our words
for a God who says
"I didn't create you
to be an actor,
there is no script,
you are not
a puppet where
I'm yanking on
your strings
every time you
miss the mark.
you are not wooden,
you are flesh,
and I put on flesh
just to look you
in the eyes and say
me too,
I get it,
and I love you."

I once heard a man say
"all love comes
with wounds and suffering
so if you really
want to know
what someone loves,
watch what they
suffer over."

and I never thought
I was worth suffering for
until I heard about
a man who died
because I
was worth saving.

and I thought
it's really kind of hard
to judge and hang
at the same time,
unless it was grace
that kept him there
or judgement
he was not
trying to pass.

-No Judgements

joy is real.
I know because
I am here.

my voice has
returned strong.
this heart has been
kissed by confidence,
revived by the story
of hopes healing.

she whispers,
"the joy of finding
something that was lost
often outweighs the joy
of receiving it
in the first place
and I have been found

living instead of existing
reconnected to peace
that passes
all understanding."

I smiled again.

-Next I'll Sing

ACKNOWLEDGEMENTS

Thank you to my Grandad for telling me, "God will be your voice" and inspiring the title of this book.

Thank you to my editor Eva Xanthopoulus for pouring over every word and identifying elements that make up my unique writing style.

Thank you to Milan DelVecchio for listening intently enough to help me illustrate what was in my heart.

Thank you to Brian Superb Poetry for constantly challenging me to write authentically.

Thank you to Kiara Imani Williams for helping me create a plan to connect every part of my writing process to a meaningful outcome.

Thank you to Daniel, for first giving me an intro to spoken-word poetry through a piece you shared about your brother in a classroom at Santa Monica College…for what you awakened inside of me…a voice I didn't even know was there…

Thank you for taking time to read and support *The Birth of Light.* If you enjoyed this book, it would mean the world to me if you left a review on Amazon sharing your thoughts. I read every review and it helps new readers discover my work.

-Michael Nelder